The Journey:
The Elements for Success, Winning and Increased Performance

"Success is a Journey, not a destination. The doing is often more important than the outcome" – Arthur Ashe

The Journey:
The Elements for Success, Winning and Increased Performance

David Harrison

PINNACLE
PERFORMANCE
2015

First Printing: 2015

ISBN 978-1-326-24372-2

Pinnacle Performance
Sheffield, S35 9YZ

www.pinnacleperformance.co.uk

Also visit our Facebook page at

https://www.facebook.com/PinnaclePerformanceSheffield

And Twitter @PinPerform

Ordering Information:
Special discounts are available on quantity purchases by corporations, associations, educators, and others. For details, contact the publisher using the email below

Book shops and wholesalers: Please contact David Harrison at pinnacleperformgmail.com.

Dedication

To my amazing wife Victoria and my princess Charlotte.

Thank you for giving me the balance needed for my Journey by being my rocks to support me while I pursue my goals; it is true what they say that behind every good man there is an amazing woman, well I am truly blessed because I have two amazing and inspirational women behind me!

Contents

Acknowledgements..vii
About the Author..viii
Preface...ix
Building Blocks, Principles and the Journey..................1
Awareness: The most Important Building Block 6
    Elements of Awareness...10
    Strategies to Improve Awareness..................................12
    How the RAF Achieve Situational Awareness.................15
Belief..16
    Links between Belief and Confidence............................21
    Strategies to Change your Beliefs................................24
Balance..28
    Plate Spinning Model...29
    To Maintain Balance..34
    To Develop Balance...36
Extend your Comfort Zone.....................................38
    Extending your Comfort Zone and Learning...................41
    Steps to Extend your Comfort Zone.............................42
Hard Work...49
    What is the "Work Ethic" Belief..................................52
    How to Increase the Work Ethic Belief 53
Control the Controllables......................................56
    Steps to Controlling the Controllables.........................58
    Military Basic Training Example (by Richard Glynn)..........63
Conclusion (Inner Core)..69
References...70

Acknowledgements

There are so many people I would like to thank that have helped and contributed to this project. The most important of these people are my wife, Victoria, and my daughter Charlotte who give me the balance and support needed on my own personal Journey. Without them this wouldn't have been possible. I also want to thank my mum and dad who are the best role models you can ask for; being creative and hardworking pays off!

I want to thank Richard Glynn for contributing to the project and giving lots of constructive feedback. I want to give personal thanks to Lee Bell who is not only a good friend who gives honest and critical feedback but a great artist and it is his picture that adorns the front cover. I would also like to give thanks to Ray Gelder and the other proof readers for providing feedback on the book and making it ready for publication. I want to give thanks to Ross Burbeary who first suggested the name for the book and to Andy Brownrigg for providing valuable feedback into the contents of the book. I also want to thank colleagues past and present who helped develop the ideas within the Journey as well as all the authors whose work I have read (there are far to mention individually).

Finally, I want to thank my current and former students and clients who provided lots of feedback on the content and the techniques within the book.

Thank you everyone!

About the Author

David is a British Association of Sport and Exercise Science (BASES) Accredited Sport and Exercise Scientist who has extensive experience of working in sport, business and education environments to help people on their Journey. He has worked in higher education for over 10 years and helped numerous students to achieve their career goals. He has a large amount of experience in elite youth football where he is Head of Psychology for elite youth players and coaches at a successful football academy. Alongside this he has worked in over 15 different sports with different athletes and with people involved in business. The clients David has worked with have gone onto achieve some amazing things on their respective Journeys. David has established Pinnacle Performance, a sport psychology consultancy company based in Sheffield, UK.

He holds a MSc Sport and Exercise Science (Psychology) and BSc(Hons) Sport Development and Coaching from Sheffield Hallam University. David has also achieved a Post Compulsory Education and Training qualification and is a Chartered Scientist through the Science Council.

In his spare time David enjoys spending time with his family, reading, growing his own vegetables and travelling.

Preface

Writing a book has always been a dream of mine, and this book is the culmination of many years' hard work. I firmly believe everyone should write and publish at least one book in their life. This book is my first and will be the first of many. It outlines what I have identified as essential elements in successful people and those people that win in sport; business and in life; or in any performance environment. I have tried to put these elements forward in a way to encapsulate these ideas in a way that people can relate to. As result the length of the book is a conscious decision not to give the reader too much information but enough to establish the basics which they can then take away to learn more if needed or desired; just enough to understand so they can move forward on their Journey. The content of this book has come from working with many high performing individuals and teams in sport, business and education. It has been influenced by the experiences I have had to date, both professionally and personally.

I have wrote the book whilst trying to maintain balance so as a result it has taken the time it has to finish. The book is self-published so every aspect of the Journey to complete it, from the initial idea to getting it to print has been down to me. This book is a living example of the importance of the elements outlined in this book. These are the elements that are needed to achieve success and reach the goals you set yourself. So, everything you do in life can be traced back to these essential elements that are called Building Blocks and Principles.

The title of any book is important and this book is called the Journey for a reason. The name came about after a conversation with a good friend of mine who happened to mention the journey as a potential name for the book after we had been talking about the process of development and improvement of elite youth football players. So the Journey is a metaphor for the never ending process of improvement which will ultimately lead to individual success. It's also a metaphor to signify that everyone's Journey is different so success and winning is relative to the individual. It turns out that it is not the destination that is the most important aspect of your Journey but how far you can go. You see and read of the different aspects of the Journey every day from elite sport to business to general everyday life which highlights their truly positive impact they can have on your life.

I have learnt so much from the process of writing this book, trying to capture the ideas I have on success in a way that is easy to pick up, read and use. The content is grounded in theory from sport, business and performance psychology but I didn't want another text book that presented the theory in an academic way. I also didn't want another self-help book from a self-styled guru, I wanted a personable book that people can read and relate to; I wanted a happy medium between the two. The Journey will allow you to improve your chances of winning in whatever you do by providing real examples and quotes from successful people to reinforce the ideas outlined within it.   It can be used as your success and performance manifesto to propel you toward your goals. To sum up the content outlined in the book there is a great military example provided by Richard Glynn at the end that really emphasizes the Building Blocks and Principles outlined in the book.

As the Journey never ends and the Building Blocks and Principles influence everything else we do this book will be the first book in a number of books around success, winning and enhanced performance. These will focus around the individual, teams and leaders in a range of performance environments.

Rich and I have also developed the Pinnacle Performance Team Development Kit to help teams and groups become more efficient to help them to be more successful; to reach their pinnacle performance. The kit embeds the Building Blocks and Principles outlined in the Journey to provide functional activities and exercises to help teams on their Journey. Check out our website (www.pinnacleperformance.co.uk) for more information on the Pinnacle Performance Team Development Kit.

If you find a copy of this book in a coffee shop, airport lounge or even a car boot sale please take a picture of yourself with the book and post it to our Facebook page (details of this can be found in the book information inside the book cover) as we want to get our message of the Journey spread far and wide (and also catalogue your Journeys and experiences!).

We also want to hear your experiences of using the book and its contents so please share these on our Facebook page as well.

There are also a number of diagrams that accompany the contents of the book and these are available on our website.

I try to practice using the Building Blocks and principles in this book, in both my personal and professional lives, it is hard work (one of the Principles outlined in the book) but so fulfilling. I want to help as many people as I can to move forward on their Journey toward success so hopefully this book can help achieve this. So the Journey is a life style, it's a decision to become the best person you can be.

On behalf, of myself and Rich we hope you enjoy the book and take a lot from it, as much as what we have taken from writing it. If you have any questions please do not hesitate to get in touch via our Facebook page or through our website.

Dave Harrison
March, 2015

"I am the master of my fate;
I am the captain of my soul."

- William Ernest Henley

Building Blocks, Principles and the Journey

This book will outline what is needed for the Journey toward success, winning and increased performance. The ideas within the book will allow you to work towards your goals and dreams to help you achieve; to achieve success on you Journey. These are the foundations that influence absolutely everything that we do and these must be in place if we are to reach and maximize our true potential. This always reminds me of a story that is popular in many primary schools where one man built his house on sand and another built his on stone. The house built on stone survived the storm but the other house was washed away. This is exactly the same if you want to be successful. Your foundations must be strong, positive and supportive to drive you forward.

"The only Journey is the one within." – Rainer Maria Rilke

There are two main reasons for writing this book. The first is that we realized that the foundations of every Journey to success and winning can be traced to 3 **Building Blocks** and 3 **Principles** that we outline these in this book. The building blocks are **Awareness**, **Belief** and **Balance** and the Principles are **Extend Your Comfort Zone**, **Hard Work** and **Control the Controllables**. These building blocks and principles are apparent in all successful people in all performance environments whether this is sport, business or education. Without these building blocks success and pinnacle performance cannot be achieved. If this book can help you identify these necessary building blocks for success then we have achieved our first objective; for you to become more aware of the starting point on your Journey to success.

The second reason for the book is to help you develop these building blocks; to give you a helping hand along your Journey. This is done through a series of tools that give you an insight into first becoming aware of the importance and impact a solid foundation has on your Journey, but then using these tools to improve your building blocks and principles. These tools should be visited regularly to ensure you are moving forward (as you would frequently sharpen your axe if you chopped wood!). This is hard work (which is one of the key principles which we will come to later in the book). Working on these building blocks is like building a house; you wouldn't expect a house to be built in one day; it takes time and lots of hard work. Or if you went out on one training run you wouldn't expect to beat Mo Farah!

So why these? Let's use a metaphor of laying a foundation to build a house to emphasize... If you were building a house you would want the best materials to build a strong solid foundation; these are the **building blocks** in the book. To make these building blocks work effectively you would need to bind these together and the ingredients for this are what we call the **principles**. We have said the building blocks are awareness, belief and balance with the principles being extending your comfort zone, hard work and control the controllables. All of these are needed before anything else to be successful in any performance environment. The principles are needed to make the building blocks work. The building blocks give the principles purpose and direction. Together the building blocks and principles are a formidable team pushing forward on your Journey. The first building block to be laid will always be Awareness. There is a diagram on our website that conceptualizes this.

For these building blocks and principles to work there is something that must be understood and accepted. This is **that the Journey to pinnacle of performance never ends** so success is to be always in a state of positive forward motion, to be always developing and striving to improve to reach the pinnacle but knowing that it can never truly be reached. In essence we are saying that the Journey is inward; focusing on you and should not focus on the outward influences in surrounding environment. This is real success. This is pinnacle performance.

"Focus on the Journey, not the destination." – Greg Anderson

If you focus on the Journey then the destination is inconsequential. As long as you are always putting one step in front of the other and no matter how small the steps you are taking you are moving forward, working towards pinnacle performance. It is essential you understand and are comfortable with this. We are programmed as Human beings to focus on the destination of the Journey; the end results of our work and the tasks we complete. However, when we look beyond this at the actual Journey and the individual steps we need to take the destination tends to take care of itself and before we know it we reached and even surpassed it.

"After climbing a great hill, one only finds that there are many more hills to climb." - Nelson Mandela

The first of the building blocks is **awareness**. Being truly aware is difficult (and hard work!) but we will highlight what awareness is, its importance along with strategies you can put in place to become more aware. You're already becoming more aware just by reading this book! This leads onto the first principle that runs throughout the book and this is **hard work**. The building blocks of pinnacle performance require large degrees of hard work and time to first recognize their importance and then to improve and streamline them to move forward on your Journey.

"The first step toward change is awareness. The second step is acceptance." - Nathaniel Branden

Being aware and working hard is extremely important but is useless unless you add the other building blocks into the mix. Once you are aware you need to get yourself moving. To do this you need to believe you can move and keep moving. So this takes us to the second building block ... **belief**. Belief is behind everything that we do. You may think you are moving forward on your Journey but there may be a limiting belief that is slowing you down or even stopping you. Positive and strong beliefs drive you forward and if you can remove or change the negative beliefs then

The Sheffield College
Hillsborough LRC
Telephone: 0114 260 2254

you will be surprised how much momentum you can pick up on your Journey.

The second principle within this book is **to extend your comfort zone**; taking you from a point of being comfortable to a place beyond this which allows us to grow and move forward. This is a key principle in your Journey and is something we urge you to implement; to be conscious of always trying to extend your comfort zone. Do this and you are moving on your Journey towards pinnacle performance and as a result the principle of extending your comfort zone is an extremely powerful principle. You need to actively seek the very edge of your comfort zone and then go that one step further. This is the only way you can improve and be successful.

So you have the building blocks of awareness, and belief, the last building block needed is **balance**. All laws of nature support this as a building block as everything in nature is working to establish balance. If everything in your life is balanced then you can generate maximum force for your Journey. If you have balance then everything is moving and pushing in the right direction then you will able to travel further. So by being aware you may realize that one aspect of your life is unbalanced and causing you to not generate as much force to move forward as you need. You can then work to regain balance in that aspect of your life. Think of yourself as a car, if one wheel isn't balanced it will pull in that direction which will eventually cause the car to crash or for another part of the car to eventually break.

The final principle is your ability to **control the controllables**. This sounds easier than it actually is because there is a natural tendency to focus on things that are not in our control. Test yourself for an hour or even a day and just count how many times you talk or think of things outside of your control. For example you might say "the weather is rubbish today" (British people love to talk about the weather!) when you can't control the weather (How great would this be during a British Summer?!); you can only control your reaction to the weather. So everything outside of your control is irrelevant so the time and energy spent on these factors will be wasted. This time could be used on the things you can control to keep you moving forward. This comes back to your awareness.

There is a magnitude of literature, examples and case studies available that reinforces these building blocks of pinnacle performance and the principles running around them. These are apparent if you pick up an autobiography from a successful person. This book puts these together in a different way than other books. By picking up and reading this book you are already on your Journey, because you are already making yourself aware of what you need to do to improve. The book is laid out by with the 3 building blocks presented first, then the 3 principles after and finishing on an example than emphasizes how the building blocks and principles work together.

Let's take a look at each building block and principle.

"The Journey of a thousand miles begins with one step." – Lao Tzu

Awareness: The most Important Building Block

Awareness is absolutely essential in your Journey toward success and pinnacle performance. Awareness has been highlighted so many times as a key indicator of success in a range of performance environments and is the most important building block to have in place before looking at any others (you need to be aware you need to work on something before you work on it!). Every other skill, quality and task can always be traced back to awareness. So it's like the first brick a builder places when they are laying foundations to build a wall; every other brick is linked to this first one.

"Start where you are. Use what you have. Do what you can." – Arthur Ashe

In the modern world there are an infinite number of things happening and all these interact and influence everything else. Being aware of this is important as successful people are aware of how things interact but only focus on the things that are pertinent to their Journey and they disregard everything else, the principle of control the controllables. Improved awareness will have a dramatic and positive effect on your Journey toward pinnacle performance.

If you are more aware then you are able to develop the necessary knowledge that will allow you to work towards improving which in turn leads to being more successful. Increased awareness gives you the knowledge to develop **'next action thinking'** (more on this in the strategies to improve section below) but you also need the principle of extending your comfort zone to allow you to implement this correctly. This will also be supported by the principle of hard work. Being aware is hard work because you have to assign time to constantly look at what you do. You also need to break the elements of awareness down (See the elements of awareness section) to refine and improve what you do. So for example in business if you were working on a key contract to take your business to the next level of operation then it is hard work to become aware of all the potential things you need to and how they interact for you and your business to achieve your objective of improving the business.

The process of breaking down the elements of awareness requires constant vigilance; you need to become a sponge and seek out information and experiences that will provide you with an opportunity to learn. This will highlight what constitutes success in your environment and then you can implement appropriate strategies related to this to move forward. The key to this vigilance is being specific. Awareness allows you to become proactive rather than reactive but you need to be specific to really break down and peel away to what is really required. When you become aware of something that is important you will want to know absolutely everything about it. This gives you the opportunity to identify how this will work and interact with everything else on your Journey. Once you have identified an important aspect that you need to be aware of, work to break this down even more. You can do this by being critical by using effective questioning (more on this in the strategies to improve awareness section) which will improve your knowledge and understanding so you can use it to move you toward on your Journey.

You can expect becoming aware to be time consuming as seeking out the elements that are required to drive us forward need to be identified, understood how and why they needed and then finally strategies need to be used to use this knowledge effectively to improve. Just starting the process will begin to break these elements down to start to increase your knowledge and understanding. This requires persistence to keep focused on the key things that will drive you forward on your Journey. However the downside to this process is that it can be tiring as you are constantly on the edge of your comfort zone (more on this later) seeking out new knowledge and understanding. Being aware will keep you on the edge of our comfort zone and will also allow you to develop as this is the best place to be. We learn more when we are uncomfortable.

"Move out of your comfort zone. You can only grow if you are willing to feel awkward and uncomfortable when you try something new." – Brian Tracy

You need to get the balance right between being on the edge of your comfort zone and stepping over which could cause your focus to go astray. Becoming aware should be a gradual process to allow you to become accustomed to the most important things you have identified that will drive you forward before seeking additional knowledge.

Being engaged in the process of becoming aware to identify and then gain knowledge can become obsessive. Being obsessive can be both positive and negative. It is a real positive because it provides the focus and drive to have the need to know and study everything in that area. This increased attention can catapult you forward on your Journey. This obsession to improve can be seen in cycling with Team Sky. Sir Dave Brailsford (Team Sky Principal) has coined a term of 'marginal gains' where everyone on the team is almost obsessed with looking for small improvements which when combined equate to increased time gains for riders and thus ultimately success in major competitions (Olympics and consecutive Tour De France wins). The negative of this process is that it can ultimately affect your balance (more on balance later) as you neglect other aspects of your life.

"We're often so busy cutting through the undergrowth we don't even realize we're in the wrong jungle." - Stephen Covey

A major positive in the process of becoming aware is that it allows you to take stock of where you are on your Journey which highlights whether you are heading in the right direction. As Stephen Covey, in his book *The 7 Habits of Highly Effective People* (I would highly recommend this book), suggested people work so hard and invest so much time on what they think is their preferred destination that they become blinkered. They try to force the continuation of their Journey in the wrong direction instead of stopping to change direction to a new more preferred destination. As you work to become more aware you may come to realize that your chosen destination for your Journey isn't the destination you really need to reach to achieve pinnacle performance. If this is the case then you need to employ next action thinking which will initiate actions to change your Journey to your preferred destination. For example people who have started a particular career path realize that this is not for them as they are aware they are not happy so they take action and enroll on a course at college that will change their career destination.

As with anything there are negatives so you need to be mindful (and aware!) that becoming obsessive on increasing awareness and gaining as much knowledge as you can on a particular element has. As this takes a large amount of time with the focus on getting knowledge you can take your eye off other things (see balance section). This obsession is a particular negative if you, as Covey suggests, are "in the wrong jungle" because working hard to get to your destination in the wrong jungle is fruitless as no amount of knowledge and time spent working hard will ever move you any closer to pinnacle performance.

To prevent this obsession you need complete separation from the process of awareness from time to time to ensure you don't burn out. The process of awareness is tiring and hard work so complete separation from the process recharges your batteries and improves your balance (more on this later). It improves balance as it allows you to dip in to focus on different elements rather than the becoming aware of one specific aspect. This in itself reduces the level of obsession whilst enjoying other things.

Here is an example of awareness in a team environment. If you are a team leader you should be aware and have knowledge of your team. So a team leader needs to be aware of a number of different elements to achieve success. These include your motivation and goals as a team leader, the different personalities of team members, their working style preferences, individual and team strengths as well as their weaknesses, however, this is not an exhaustive list. Once you know these elements you can start to implement strategies to improve these using 'next action thinking'. When you are aware of and know about these elements you can set out strategies to help the team achieve their goals and objectives. This will also reduce conflict with the team members as you are aware of what is needed to be successful by matching the team members' strengths to roles and tasks to complete the task effectively.

"An unexamined life is not worth living." –Socrates

Elements of Awareness

There are just 3 elements you need to be aware of to understand everything (I mean everything!) in your life. If you are aware of just these 3 elements you will gain massive amounts of information that you can use to improve in the different aspects of your life. This concept of just 3 elements of awareness has been around for 1000's of years which has been applied by hundreds of people in a range of performance environments. This idea was initially written about by Sun Tzi in the Art of War (around 500BC) and is still used extensively in business, sport and the military today.

These 3 elements are:

1. **You**. You are the most important tool on your Journey so learn to use your strengths effectively. For example a craftsman becomes a master of their tools; a chef becomes a master of using knives to prepare food. So you need to be aware of you, your strengths and weaknesses, your personality, your motivations and drives, your targets, objectives and goals. It also allows you to understand how you react and deal with experiences that come

up. Self-awareness will allow you to focus on your strengths whilst developing strategies to improve your weaknesses when dealing with experiences you have.

2. The **Environment**. You need to be aware of everything in the environment to understand what constitutes success and failure within it. From a football (soccer) example the things within the environment that a footballer needs to be aware of are; team mates, coaches, the opposition, ball and, the pitch conditions. So ask yourself what are the important things to focus on in your environment? Are there any relationships between people that need to be developed? Removed? How do you fit into the 'bigger picture of the environment?' Are there any unique factors in the environment that by understanding them will give you the best chance of success?

3. The **Enemy**. Not literally! However, you need to understand that there are other people competing within the same environment for the same things that you are so you need to know the strengths and weaknesses of your competition and how you compare to them. What makes you unique that allows you to achieve and be successful? What is your story? How does this make you stand out from the competition?

Another football (soccer) to use as an example are managers like Jose Mourinho who produce extensive dossiers on every opponent so that they are aware of their strengths and which areas they can exploit so they can plan effectively and maximise their chances of winning. The same can be said for Sir Alan Sugar in business who is aware and understands the unique characteristics of his business and the environment it is in. Both Jose Mourinho and Sir Alan Sugar are extremely aware which makes them successful!

Your awareness and knowledge will drive your planning which in return will maximize productivity (by employing **next action thinking**) on your Journey. Awareness is all well and good but is pretty much useless unless it is acted upon. It's very easy to improve and can be started immediately.

Strategies to Improve Awareness

1. **Use Effective Questioning**: Awareness can be increased by questioning the information you have at your disposal. Take on a childlike inquisitiveness and when you identify something that is important question it. For example my little girl always says "Daddy I have a question" and Daddy why does this happen?" So start to peel away and get more information by using the question words of what, where, when, why, how. This will lead to more knowledge and so greater awareness.

2. **Read, Watch and Observe**: Open up your senses and become a sponge, soaking up all the information you can. Read publications about your environment, read books about self – development. Try to read every day and if you do you will join a very small group of the population. Regular reading has such a dramatic effect on your awareness whilst at the same time has also been shown to reduce the risk of mental illness (A win win!). So, read everything you can about developing yourself and your environment. Also watch and observe role models in the environment you want to be successful in and watch documentaries around the subject you want to become more aware of. This will give insights into how others have been successful which you can model your future actions on. From an individual view notice how you react to certain situations and then use questioning to identify the reason why. However, be sure to question everything you read, watch and observe to ensure you are maximising your awareness as this will give you additional questions to answer.

3. **Listen**: Make sure you listen to people within your environment to gain an understanding of who they are and what information they can provide. As a result this is an extremely important strategy. Everyone should have a number of mentors (for example I have mentors for the personal and professional aspects of my life who I trust and respect with whom I can approach when I need to seek information or advice) who listen to your concerns, queries and questions and who can pass on advice of how they succeeded in their environment. So seek out and approach people who you trust and respect. You have to be able to work with them so they can pass on critical information as they will provide a sounding block to help you gain an understanding of the environment.

4. **Understand**: After reading, watching, observing and listening (points 2 and 3 above) to increase your awareness you need to spend time to understand how all the things you are now aware of interact and influence each other to effect on your Journey. This is a continuous process of learning and understanding. Where possible write down in a journal the interaction and influence of these things you are aware of and make changes as you become more aware. As well as a journal I write my understanding of things in the pinnacle performance blog.

5. **Next action thinking**: This is such a powerful strategy to increase understanding of the things you need to do to move forward on your Journey. To start, use questioning (point 1) to identify what is the very next action. So awareness will give you the information for the next action thinking by making you aware of the VERY next thing you need to do to move forward. For example, if you are aware that you struggle to get up early to go and exercise then this may point to the need that you need a training partner. So the very next action is to identify potential partners and then find their telephone number. The action after this will

then be to call them. The key here is to break up actions you come up with into very specific next actions. From this example you can't ring to ask someone to be your training partner if you don't have their telephone number! I have found people can struggle with this as they are not specific enough or don't have enough awareness of what the next action is. Next action thinking is based on a concept devised by David Allen in relation to productivity (I recommend his book Getting Things Done).

6. **Brainstorm**: After using all the strategies above undertake a brainstorming exercise. This is similar to a technique used in sport and business called Performance Profiling. Make sure you brainstorm on BIG paper. A roll of lining paper or the reverse of some old wall paper is ideal; just make sure it's nothing smaller than A3. Basically this is because the human brain works best when it can see everything in one place and the bigger paper the more compelled your brain is to fill it. As a result you get more ideas and lessen the chance of missing that key aspect that you need to be aware of. After you have got your big paper get a quiet and relaxed room where you can concentrate and not get distracted (make sure you turn off your phone and other technology!). Write down everything to come into your head. Just start writing and don't worry how it looks you can organise the information later. Use lines to join up related concepts and ideas. Use questioning to get more understanding to unpick what you are already aware of and understand (use your journal as a starting point). A good brain storming session will take place in the morning when you are fresh from a good night's sleep. The session should not last longer than an hour (I use a 30 minute egg timer and when this is done I leave the exercise to come back to it later for another 30 minutes which allows my brain the time to make sense of what has been written down whilst continuing to work on the ideas in the sub conscious). When you are finished keep the paper; you can add to it later or come back to the

ideas at a later date. These papers should become living and evolving documents. If possible leave the paper out so you can add things you come up with after the session. The brain doesn't think in a logical way and will come up with things at different often peculiar times. When you are asked to think and be creative on the spot your brain can't do it. It can take time to warm up to consider ideas plus it doesn't think in a logical way. Think back to the last time you lost your keys, your brain will give you answer when you least expect it! For me it is days later when I am in the shower!

Remember: To start with developing awareness and knowledge of the things you can control as an individual.

How the RAF achieve Situational Awareness

In crisis and conflict situations, high quality, up to date information is required to enable effective decision-making. Understanding the situation demands enhanced situational awareness. The RAF achieves this by using its multiple assets. So in the first instance this is achieved by Drone and Satellite surveillance capability. To add further information high-resolution video images can be provided by combat aircraft. These can now be data-linked directly to soldiers on the ground through lap-top terminals. This technique is particularly useful in providing accurate situational awareness.

Belief

"Belief in oneself is one of the most important bricks in building any successful venture" – Lydia M. Child

Self-belief is the **most important aspect** of being successful in sport, business and education. Without it you would not be able to reach and then maintain pinnacle performance so when self-belief is added to awareness you are starting to get a strong foundation for the Journey forward. Your beliefs are based on your personality, experiences and relationships you have had throughout your life. For example, I have a belief that creativity is an important part of the things you do. I believe that doing things differently is something that should be encouraged, to be a shepherd and not a sheep and to stand out from the crowd. This belief originated from my parents, my mum who is very creative and my dad, who is very much not influenced by the opinions of others. This belief evolved from my observations of people who were different and stood out, these were individuals who didn't conform on some level with social norms and at the same time were not concerned with the opinions of others. Standing out from the crowd can be difficult growing up so a strong belief that this is the right thing to maintain individuality was needed.

Your beliefs will have shaped who you are as a person, your skills and qualities and influence ALL your actions and experiences. Beliefs are linked to your story, which is the story of your Journey so far. This story makes you unique (no one else has had the same Journey as you!) but it is your interpretation of the experiences you have had so far that shape, influence and form your beliefs. Your story is who you are as a person so as a result beliefs are deep rooted in your inner core (more on this later) so these are difficult to change but can slowly be changed with the principles of hard work and extending your comfort zone. This starts with changing your interpretation of your story; your story is a New York Times best seller!

Your beliefs are internal and consistent, they don't change easily, your beliefs are stable, and this is who you are; the real you because your beliefs are deep rooted in the inner core (more on this at the end of the book). Your beliefs can sometimes be subconscious influencing your actions without you even being aware of them. Your beliefs influence every aspect of your life whether that is personally, professionally or socially. As a result it's really important that you are aware of them. When you understand them and how they influence your behavior you can start to implement strategies to change any beliefs that are inhibiting your performance.

Awareness helps you understand who you are and what your beliefs are and their influence.

Beliefs take a long time to change, and awareness is the first step. Constantly revisit your beliefs through the awareness exercises from the previous section to challenge your beliefs and to understand their influence. This will allow your beliefs to change slowly over time; imagine a large glacier moving slowly down a mountain.

Beliefs are formed in just two ways. They are either formed slowly over time or as a result of a one off specific painful or pleasurable experience. To emphasize the forming of beliefs slowly over time lets imagine a roof that is gradually leaking. The drips of water from this leak left unchecked will soon form mold on the paint on the wall! So looking back at my belief around creativity and standing this developed through watching my mum being creativity and the interactions of my dad with people who had different opinions to him and his steadfast belief that he wouldn't be influenced by these opinions if he disagreed with them.

Beliefs formed from a one off event are like phobias people can have. For example, someone may have developed a belief that all flying creatures are dangerous (even though they are not!)

when, as a child, a flock of birds flew off together when the person was in close proximity. Whichever way beliefs are formed they become stable and start to consciously and/or unconsciously influence your behavior and actions. As they are stable they take a long time to change irrespective of how they are formed.

Beliefs can be viewed like the table in your kitchen or living room. The table top is held in place and its weight taken by the table legs to form a solid stable structure. Different tables have different designs (any trip to Ikea will show this!); there are the traditional tables with 4 legs but there are also tables that have more or less than the traditional 4 legs. So, if we see the table top as the belief there needs to be legs to hold it in place; let's call these **reference points**. These reference points are very similar to the legs of your dining room table. They will keep the table top (Belief) stable and secure. The stronger reference points or the more of them there are the more stable the belief. Beliefs need to be positive to drive you forward on your Journey to pinnacle performance. When you have a positive belief you need to use it to your advantage and work hard to maintain its positive influence (a little bit like polishing your table?!) so it continues to work in your favor.

An example here would be a golfer who has developed a belief that an aspect of their game is incredibly strong through using the 1000's of practice shots they have taken that have been successful. These reference points are supported by the reference points they have gained in major golf tournaments around this particular aspect of their game. When the reference points are combined they provide solid support for the golfer's positive belief for that particular aspect which pushes them forward on their Journey to success.

Beliefs can also be negative and hold you back. If this is the case then you need to change your table! To do this you start by identifying new positive reference points which will, when strong be able to hold in place a strong positive belief. By identifying and developing new reference points you make the existing belief unstable as the old reference points are no longer strong enough to support the existing belief. This is because your focus is on the new positive beliefs, thus it is no longer needed and so is removed (I always imagine taking the legs off my mum's dining room table and then replacing it with a new table!). As a result a new positive belief is formed as the new reference points reinforce this new belief. For example, a business owner might have had some bad experiences where his confidence may have affected his negotiations in finalizing business deals, which then contributed to their belief that they shouldn't be in business as they are not good enough. For this to change focus needs to be on the times when their confidence allowed deals to be closed and then to use these as reference points along with using other aspects of business where they are particularly strong as reference points to produce a new positive belief that they should be in business and are good at it.

We now know your beliefs influence everything you do so these beliefs must be positive to feed your actions and propel you forward on your Journey. Like the plant food you give your house plant which stimulates growth to allow the plant to make the best of the window sill you have placed it on. Without this plant food the plant would just exist and not thrive. Like the plant on your window sill your beliefs need to be fed regularly by the strong positive **reference points** that maintain it. So self-belief needs to be fed constantly with positive reference points to maintain its position otherwise it will inhibit or even stop you from moving forward. Positive reference points that are reinforced regularly give a stronger belief. Therefore be an optimist and concentrate on your strengths; be a glass half full person (but you first need to be aware of your strengths!).

"A pessimist sees the difficulty in every opportunity; an optimist sees the opportunity in every difficult." – Winston Churchill.

Be aware of your beliefs that need development but focus on your beliefs that are your strengths. Using sport as an example, in training athletes should focus on areas of development but in competition focus on their strengths. So in your environment identify times where you can focus on your beliefs that need development, like an athlete, this is your training. In times where you need to compete to be successful, like a job interview, focus on your strength's to maximize your chances of success and to keep moving forward on your Journey. In both your training and competition work on developing and strengthening your positive reference points to increase the stability of your positive beliefs.

Your references points can be developed and strengthened by words you use to define the experiences within your environment. The words you use have an extremely powerful effect on your beliefs which, as a result, influence everything you do. The words that you use to describe your beliefs are like the plant food you give your house plant. So use positive words to describe your story as these will eventually become positive reference points which will then form positive beliefs that drive you forward on your Journey. So words make reference points. You are what your words say you are. **You have control**. So feed your beliefs with positive words.

"Beliefs have the power to create and the power to destroy." - Tony Robbins

Successful people in all performance environments have strong positive beliefs that are the driving force behind their success. There are stories of successful athletes who had such positive beliefs when they were developing as an athlete that this drove them onto become Olympic Champion or a World Cup Winner. Their belief that they were going to be a successful athlete was so strong and powerful it allowed them to maintain their Journey to winning despite the numerous obstacles that they encountered along the way. Imagine the athlete to be a captain of a ship sailing on the ocean while their positive strong belief they have is the compass to assist them moving forward on their

Journey by maintaining the right course. To plot the right course for their beliefs the athletes constantly used positive words to feed their references points for their positive beliefs so that these beliefs reminded stable and secure which allowed the athlete to use the belief positivity on their Journey. They would very rarely use negative language that prevented negativity creeping into their reference points which would then weaken their beliefs. Any negativity that did invariably creep in was quickly stopped and converted to a positive reference point (a technique known as reframing, and there will be more on this later in the strategies to change your belief section) because any negativity would ultimately remove the positive belief as it weakened the reference points that held the belief in place.

Reference points are something which we can ultimately control (remember the principle of control the controllables, so see this section later in the book). Reference points that are out of our control or any that we can only influence (e.g. winning a football match or other people's actions!) should be avoided. So because beliefs influences every aspect of your life we can slowly change belief from the outside into the inner core where your beliefs live by establishing and maintaining strong reference points.

So let's take confidence for example.

Links between Belief and Confidence

Confidence is important in the Journey to pinnacle performance but is underpinned by a strong positive belief that goals can be achieved despite knowing with 100% certainty that there will be ups AND downs in everything we do. So a positive belief is ultimately demonstrated in showing confidence which will get you through the downs that you have on your Journey. Confidence is, however, very subjective. This means that a positive reference point for one person that gives them confidence can be a negative reference point for someone else and reduce their confidence. So what gives confidence for one person will cause another person to lose confidence. Think back to the table metaphor that we used when we discussed beliefs above, everyone would have a different ideal belief table top and reference point table legs to support their belief. As a result there is a clear link between beliefs and confidence because positive beliefs are demonstrated by having confidence in what you do. If you have strong positive beliefs then you will be more confident. As you demonstrate more confidence you strengthen the beliefs that underpin this confidence, it's a positive cycle relationship between confidence and beliefs.

The confidence you exhibit in different environments can be an indication of your beliefs (positive or negative) so an awareness of your confidence in different areas will allow you initiate strategies to change or reinforce these beliefs. Strengthening your beliefs will have positive and dramatic effect on your confidence but this will take time. This is because confidence is more superficial than your beliefs so this can be influenced and changed easier than you beliefs (there is a diagram on our website); so increasing your confidence will slowly start to have a positive effect on your beliefs.

We can control our confidence; it's within our control, we can manage it because it is subjective so can increase and decrease quickly but importantly you control it. Confidence is linked to your beliefs by your positive references points so positive strong references points provide positive beliefs which are demonstrated in high levels of confidence. For example during a wedding reception the best man maybe confident speaking to an audience as he has positive reference points from his career as a teacher whereas the father of the groom may not be confident because he is a builder and does not have any reference points to get confidence from (this would be the same if you asked the best man to build a wall, he won't have a clue because he hasn't any reference points to call upon!).

You can be confident in one situation but not others; this is contagious so it must be managed so it has a positive effect and not hold you back. This management can be improved by gaining more experience in the environment that you want to be confident in. Through awareness you can highlight positive reference points that you can you use to support your beliefs from these experiences. As a result one way to develop belief is to work on your confidence. Start with an environment that you are comfortable with to identify reference points that are positive and demonstrate your confidence. As confidence is contagious you can start to use the confidence you have in one environment to one where you don't feel as comfortable (this will slowly extend your comfort zone; more on this later!).

There are two types of confidence. In sport these are Training Confidence and Match Confidence. The first is being confident in training. Training is a safe and comfortable environment where there is less pressure and more freedom to play. Match confidence is confidence to get the job done in a competitive environment. There are lots of uncertainties in competition due to the influences of some many things that are out of the control of the athlete. This results in more pressure which it is less comfortable because we like comfort and to be in control. So you can be confident in one but not the other until you get experience in both. However confidence from one can be taken from one and used in the other if you have limited experience. For example a youth footballer could use their training confidence to use it in their competitive first team debut. Remember that the confidence that a player has is underpinned and influenced by the beliefs they have. So, the youth player in the above example must have a positive belief to demonstrate confidence in their debut. This can be applied to your situation. Take your confidence from one area that you are comfortable with and highlight positive reference points to support this. Then use these in a situation where you are not as confident and your confidence will slowly start to increase which will in turn develop a stronger belief as you have positive reference points to refer to.

There are strategies to improve confidence. The first and the most important is to get experience and learn from them; make sure you are always look to extend your comfort zone (more on this later).

"Get Comfortable being uncomfortable." – Jillian Michaels

When gaining experiences that extend your comfort zone work on acting confident and copy role models or people who you consider to be successful in that environment by watching and observing their behavior they use to demonstrate superior confidence.

*Confidence is an extremely important aspect for the Journey to pinnacle performance and will be covered in detail in future books in the series, in the meantime check out the Pinnacle Performance blog for more insights into confidence.

Strategies to Change your Beliefs

1. **Talk and act** like the belief you want to create, play make believe with the belief you want. This will change your behavior as your beliefs find it difficult to distinguish between this 'make believe' and your real beliefs. So by changing your behavior you start to filter this towards your beliefs that are stable within the belief system in the inner core. Given enough time this 'acting' will seep into the inner core and affect a change upon the existing belief, this is similar to 'internalizing' that is often used in psychological theory. You may have done an experiment at school where you placed a piece of celery into a beaker of colored water (I think at my school we used a red color) to demonstrate how plants bring water up from the soil. When you came to check on the celery at the start of the next class the dye had moved up the piece of celery. This is the same effect when you act and talk like the belief you want to create. As in the celery experiment this takes time.

Another example to demonstrate this is the leaking roof we used above to show how beliefs are formed; it takes time for the leak in the roof to have an effect on the plaster on the wall. So, for example if you want the belief that you are a confident public speaker then you need to consistently talk and act like you are confident professional speaker.

2. To speed this process up you can reinforce the 'acting' by undertaking some intensive re - programming of your beliefs in your inner core. To do this write down the new belief you want. Repeat this 10 times and make sure you hand write these. By hand writing these new beliefs you are strengthening your commitment to them as it is in your own hand writing. It's like writing lines at school! Do this daily, twice if you can. In addition to hand writing these beliefs say the belief out loud standing in front of the mirror and looking at yourself as you read your hand written notes. If you say the new belief out loud daily as well as writing them down the re-programming of the new belief happens quicker. Saying the new belief out loud has a similar affect to writing the belief in your own hand writing; it really strengthens and reinforces the commitment to the new belief.

3. **Use positive strong words**: Think about the words you use to describe your belief or your performance and keep a diary of the words you use to describe yourself and your experiences. For one week just record the words you use and then review your entries and look to change any negative words to positive words. This is known as reframing which is a powerful technique for changing your beliefs. When you become conscious of the words you use you can start to use strong positive words to 'big up' your strengths and experiences; to exaggerate them to make strong reference points. Use these words to turn your perceived weaknesses into positive strengths that can drive you forward. If you are a small business how can you use

these strengths to your advantage? If you turn your perceived weaknesses into an advantage then are they still weaknesses? Have some fun with this. Remember you are what you say you are! A great example of this is the fantastic footballer Lionel Messi. He is not the biggest footballer but uses this to his advantage by having a lower centre of gravity which allows him to turn on a sixpence and dart past bigger defenders. He uses his smaller size as a strength which could have been considered a weakness by some.

4. Another great exercise to do to change your beliefs is to **recollect your best ever performance** and then write it down. When you write it down be as descriptive and detailed as possible. Really focus on the language that you use by using strong positive words to really place emphasis on your strengths and to make your perceived weaknesses into strengths. Think back to Lionel Messi and the descriptive he would use as he is weaving in between defenders. This will make strong reference points that you can use to change your belief. Do this exercise regularly, rewrite once a week and re - read it every day, Make sure you read it *every day!*

5. A belief is maintained by the number of reference points you associate with it. So complete the **Table Top Exercise**. Imagine your belief as the table top and the reference points are the table legs. If you have strong table legs (reference points) then you will have a strong table top (belief). To remove the table top we have to remove the table legs and then get a new table! As a result, to form a new table (belief) we have to put in place enough legs that are strong enough to hold this belief. Using the strategies above will start to break down the table legs which are your reference points that hold inhibiting beliefs. Then imagine that these reference points have wood worm which will slowly eat away at them to weaken them and the existing beliefs they hold in place (the effect of using the strategies

above). These exercises will then start to produce a new table top as a new belief as positive reference points can't hold an inhibiting belief. For new beliefs we have to get new reference points (legs). So completing these strategies above repeatedly will create the new belief (table top). An example to emphasize this would be if you were to construct a flat pack dining table (we all love building flat pack furniture!) you would want matching legs (reference points) to support and match the table top (belief). If you found the legs or table top to be different you would take the whole thing back to the store. This is exactly the same with your beliefs; they must match the reference points you provide. This concept originated from Anthony Robbins book "Awaken the Giant Within" (I would wholeheartedly recommend this book and would place this book in my top five books of all time).

Balance

Mother Nature is a good place to start when it comes to looking at the importance of balance. In nature everything is constantly working to try and achieve and then maintain balance, if one thing is out of kilt then, within the environment, nature will work to try to restore balance (this may take days, months, years or even millennia!). In your body everything within it is working to maintain equilibrium (a big word from biology!) which is essentially means balance. This is done through a process called homeostasis (another big word!) whereby, for example, you may eat or do something and your body automatically responds by doing something to return the body to balance or equilibrium.

"Man maintains his balance, poise, and sense of security only as he is moving forward." – Maxwell Maltz

Another example, imagine walking or running for the bus; you wouldn't get anywhere if you weren't' balanced. You would fall over and miss the bus! When you learn to walk as a child there are lots to focus on because it's a complicated action for a small child so you can easily miss or forget a key factor (like putting your next foot forward!) and your balance is gone and you fall over! This is true for life as a whole. You have to remain balanced so balance is another key building block in our Journey toward pinnacle performance. Everyone is different consequently the balance that works for you will not work for someone else. You need to identify and find the balance that fits you and your Journey.

"Just as your car runs more smoothly and requires less energy to go faster and farther when the wheels are in perfect alignment, you perform better when your thoughts, feelings, emotions, goals, and values are in balance." – Brian Tracy

With regards to balance see yourself like a car which needs everything to be running smoothly for the car to run efficiently. You need to understand the many parts that make you as a person and how they interact with the environment and the key people within it. This goes back to awareness and what your beliefs are relating to these key aspects in the environment; this is a key factor to maintain balance. Imagine you were going through some difficulties at home. A part of you is out of balance. Would you be fully efficient within your job? How long would it be before you fell and stopped moving forward?

Think of all the roles, responsibilities and positions you have and the beliefs you have around each of these. There will be more of these than you think with some of these having multiple layers. For example you may be a parent so what are your beliefs around parenting, do these match what you are currently doing? If not you might be off balance and not moving forward on your Journey. All these roles can be placed in whole person wheel (there is a diagram of this on the website as an example) and from there you can divide the circle into the time you devote to each role. Again consider how the amount of time you currently give to each role to your beliefs you have. Back to the parent role; does the time you assign for being a parent mirror the beliefs that you have for this role? Are you spending enough time with your family?

"I believe that being successful means having a balance of success stories across the many areas of your life. You can't truly be considered successful in your business life if your home life is in shambles." – Zig Ziglar

Plate spinning Model

Think of a plate spinner at the circus. If one plate is struggling, the plate spinner has to see to that plate and whilst they are doing this they have to leave other plates which could then start to wobble and potentially fall! So the circus plate spinner has too constantly move between all of their plates to keep them spinning. Each one of the roles, responsibilities and projects you have can be viewed as an individual plate. You will have plates spinning at home, socially and at work. All these different plates spin at different speeds and are individual to you. Everyone is different; some people need to spin their family plate move than others, this goes back to awareness and understanding what works for you as an individual. So, if one plate starts to wobble then you need to be aware of this and work hard (a principle later in the book) to restore the balance whilst maintaining the spinning of all the other plates you have.

On top of understanding you and the plates you have you need to understand and be aware of the important people within your environment. For example I need to be aware of the plates my wife and little girl (she seems to have a better social life than her mum and dad!) have to understand my environment to make it as conducive and balanced as I can for the Journey of myself and my family. A very important note here; we can't control other people (see the control the controllables section later in the book) but we can be aware of them and potentially influence them. Additionally, we have to get balance ourselves first before anything else which involves an awareness of outside influences such as these important people. You need to consider what their beliefs are, what impact they might have on you and your situation so be aware of this to improve balance in your immediate environment. Consider what their strengths are and areas they need to improve? What makes them tick? What motivates them? What are their goals? Add to the mix that each one of these important people will have their individual plates spinning, some maybe out of control and some more than others. You need to become aware of these to get balance within yourself. What strategies can you employ to work with someone to get you back on the Journey to pinnacle performance? There may be times where difficult decisions have to be made if you realize you can't work with that person or you aren't moving forward on the Journey with them in your life.

Remember: The Journey to pinnacle performance is about you moving forward first and foremost but also those close and important to you. You might as well have some company on your Journey! So once you have mastered the strategies outlined in this book to develop the building blocks and principles pass these onto others. This helping of others will reinforce the building blocks and principles for yourself but will also develop them in others which will move you even further on your Journey. It's a win win situation. By helping you are moving other people forward on their Journey whilst at the same time propelling yourself even further on your Journey.

So on your Journey you need to be able to juggle and keep spinning your own plates but you also need to become aware of the plates of others within your environment as well. Therefore, there are lots of plates to focus on and keep spinning, but, finally we need to add one more variable to the mix. To add to the difficulty of spinning your own numerous plates, being aware of other people's plates the plates you need to spin are all in different places! It's like having plates spinning in different rooms. You need to be able to regularly visit these rooms and the plates within them. For example some of your plates will be at home, some maybe at your place of work. To move forward on your Journey you need to balance you and all the different parts of you (family, home, education, hobbies, social etc) which may be housed in different places.

So when one of these plates is struggling (starting to wobble!) your efficiency and effectiveness will start to be effected inhibiting your performance on your Journey. To prevent this from happening make regular visits to each of your plates to give them a spin. By this I mean spend time with them to improve and work on them but be aware that different plates spin at different speeds so you may need to spend longer on some than others. Also be aware of those plates that maybe out of sight like those at work or the office; they are in a different room. So keep regular checks on them and give them a spin by spending time with them as required.

Whilst at work and within the workplace think about the balance needed to be a success for yourself, the organization and teams that you are part of. Do you need to be close to people at work socially to be successful to get the results you want? Will this closeness between you and your colleagues fit the balance needed or required by the organization? With regard to the organization you need to be aware of and balance the objectives and expectations of the organization with those of yourself. Identify what these objectives are by researching the company, the position in the market and long term plans. Don't be afraid to ask your superiors and colleagues. They will usually welcome this and be happy to speak you. Also make sure you read any company publications to get the full picture. If your expectations don't mirror those of the organization then you may have a decision to make!

Overall that's a lot plates to balance and to look after whilst also visiting different rooms to spin them! You have to find the balance that fits you as a person, the important people in your environment and any organizations you are part of. Everyone is different and every scenario is different so what will work in one scenario will not work with another.

In a perfect world (we know there is no such thing but the Journey to pinnacle performance is as close to perfect as you can get!) your plates would be housed in rooms where you have easy access to them so you are free to enter these rooms whenever you want. This would allow you to balance your plates more freely as you are able to access them and give them the time needed to keep spinning before leaving the room to spin other plates. This is hard work (a section on this is later in the book) as you have to work to keep the doors open to your different rooms to effectively keep you plates spinning.

Remember to recognize that there will be occasions when some of your plates need to spin faster than other plates. For example this could be the build up to a major sports competition (like the World Cup!) or an important business presentation deadline approaching for a million pound contract. When this happens try to foresee it and spend time on your other plates before and after to maintain balance. You must ensure that other plates are checked whilst you are working hard on one plate. If you spend too much on one plate and it continues for a prolong period of time then productivity and efficiency on your Journey could be affected. Worse still it could affect other important plates so work hard to maintain balance.

However failure to keep your doors open will eventually cause individual plates to fall and break which will then ultimately cause entire rooms to be lost. Imagine a tree at the start of autumn. The leaves of the tree start to fall off first. These are your individual plates. If it was prolonged and cold autumn and winter the branches of the tree will start to die off. These are your rooms. So it is essential you keep the doors open to the rooms you have but once you are in the room to concentrate solely on the plates within that room. This can be difficult with advances in technologies where your office email is on your mobile phone. There is a diagram on our website where you will see an example of someone focusing solely on the plates within their job role at work and failing to spin the plates of the family; which is an imperative area of any person on the Journey and these plates must be kept spinning as they help to keep everything else in balance. In this diagram the door has been closed or the person has chosen not to enter the room (back to control the controllables!) for some time. Eventually, the person may lose plates within the family and could cause the family to break off. This is not a good position for someone working toward pinnacle performance as the family provides essential support, guidance and structure needed on the Journey. Once connection to an individual room or plates has been lost it is very difficult and takes a lot of hard work to repair and re-establish the link.

You may inadvertently focus on an individual plate. Doing this will have the same effect as if you neglected a room. Eventually the connection will be lost with your other plates and you will be left spinning a solitary plate which on its own will not cause you to move forward. For example if your sole attention was on spinning the plate within the family room that was concerned with having a good time and neglected other plates (like the finances plate!) that are needed to spin in conjunction with this plate then you will eventually lose balance and other plates will start to fall away and will be lost and you will not be able to move forward on your Journey (because we all have bills to pay!).

Just a reminder that there are a number of diagrams that show the Plate Spinning Model that conceptualizes the importance of maintaining balance and what happens if we fail to do this on our website (www.pinnacleperformance.co.uk).

To maintain balance

To achieve and maintain balance work on the following:

Personally

1. Make a conscious effort to **switch off** when you are at home or doing things other than work. Learn to leave the other rooms with plates in, if you have spent a number of hours spinning them during the day at work then they will still be spinning tomorrow so don't worry about them. Work on the plates you can and don't worry about the plates in different rooms (Control the Controllables). Try not replying to work emails and answering the work mobile outside of office hours or designated hours to spend time with your family. If you feel you have to do this then allocate a specific time that family members are aware of that you can use to dedicate yourself to doing 'work stuff'. If you allocate 30 minutes and stick to it you will be amazed how much you can get done and how good the time will be with your family before and after will be. I know this can be difficult but try and follow this advice:

"Don't become a slave to technology – manage your phone, don't let it manage you." - Sir Richard Branson

2. Learn to **compartmentalize your plates**. Get a specific time for each room that your plates are in (work, home etc). The model highlights the need to spin the plates you can when you are able to. So set a time to enter every room to spin your plates. When you compartmentalize develop a semi flexible approach that concentrates on people not things. Doing this allows you to spend time, if needed, on particular plates and then to catch up on the others at a later time. People, especially those close to you are crucial in your Journey so by concentrating on people you will forge stronger and deeper relationships and move you further on your Journey.*

3. **Maximize your time** within each of your individual rooms to give you enough time to spin all the plates within the room. Maximise productivity by employing time management techniques.*

   Sometimes the best way to maximize your time is to do less. As we may have heard sometimes less is more. So if possible concentrate on quality rather than quantity; concentrate on slowing down and doing things well. Time is our most valuable resource so don't waste it by trying to cram too much in. Enjoy the time you have.

   * There will be more information in a future book on compartmentalizing your plates and maximizing your time but in the meantime check David Allen's Getting Things Done and there are several productivity apps for smart phones that can help you achieve this in the meantime.

4. **Have downtime**. Make sure you set time aside to relax and have time to yourself doing the things that you enjoy. This will recharge your batteries and allow you to refocus so you are able enter each room with energy and enthusiasm to spin your plates. This could actually be

another plate like going to the gym. For me personally I like to spend time in my garden. However remember not to spend too much time on this plate just because you enjoy it!

Family and Job Role

1. **Communicate regularly** (these could be informal chats in the car or corridor) which is open and clear to ensure that the environment (whether in your place of work or at home) is open and receptive with everyone knowing, understanding and appreciating (Awareness again!) each other's role, commitments and responsibilities (the plates others have to spin). This makes you aware of what you need to do and the number of plates you need to spin and at what speed.

2. Have **individual and consistent time** with each of your important people to check they are balanced and moving forward but also to reinforce your balance. This is important as you will be aware of things that could crop up and assist them through any situations. Helping people on their Journey also helps propel you on your individual Journey toward pinnacle performance.

To develop Balance

There a number of ways you can develop balance.

1. **Produce a whole person wheel** to check the time you spend on each aspect (your individual plates) so that they correspond with the things that you consider to be important from your belief system. Allocate a percentage of time you spend now on each segment and then give a percentage for the ideal amount of time spent on each segment based on the beliefs that you have (obviously after you are aware of your beliefs and changed any inhibiting ones; remember a few pages ago!). If this is out

of sync then implement strategies to get a better balance between your time and your beliefs.

2. **Change the number of your plates**. If you feel you have too many plates try to reduce the number by assigning plates other people (a good example here is asking children to become involved with the chores around the house). Also ASK for assistance if you are struggling to maintain balance and learn to say 'No' so you don't take too much on until you have a comfort zone that can cope with additional plates. The word no is such an important word in maintaining balance.

3. If reducing the number of plates is impossible then **utilize time management strategies** to maximize your productivity.

4. Humans work better in **a routine**; we are creatures of habit so develop a daily and weekly routine that is **semi flexible**. Semi flexible means that things can be added and removed without causing panic and worry that some of your plates may start to slip.

As human beings we crave comfort but we are faced with a dichotomy as we work best on the very edge of our comfort zone where things can be tough and challenging. Our comfort zone is the area within which we feel a sense of security and certainty. It is an area where any actions taken have been tried and tested to ensure they are known to be safe. This supports our belief that we can or can't do something. Any belief that you have whereby you think you cannot do something is a very limiting factor but as we know these can be changed. If you change your beliefs you will extend your comfort zone and vice versa. Anyone working in a performance environment will identify that stretching your comfort zone is a significant part of self-improvement and the Journey to pinnacle performance. By slowly extending our comfort zone we realize that great things can be achieved.

"Life begins at the end of your comfort zone." - Neale Donald Walsch

Moving along our Journey is a truly great feeling and makes you feel good which gives you confidence which leads to a stronger more positive belief (refer back to the link between confidence and beliefs). These things would have been considered impossible with a smaller comfort zone but as your comfort zone increases so does your belief and the realization that you can achieve what you set out to achieve.

"The knowledge of the world is only to be acquired in the world, and not in the closet" – Lord Chesterfield

We find it easy to act on and make decisions that are a part of our everyday routine, (what to eat, when to eat, who to see that day or what we will wear) as these actions make up part of our comfort zone. We find it easier to push our comfort zone when we are younger and in good health as we are in period of rapid learning and development with routines that are not as deeply structured. We also have fewer consequences and learnt inhibitions to limit our actions but this is not to say the comfort zones cannot be extended when you older, they can as we never stop learning. In fact learning can be more rewarding as we can draw on the experiences we have had to link these to our learning (more on the links between learning and extending your comfort zone later).

"A ship is safe in harbor, but that's not what ships are for." –
William Shedd

What the books on the subject don't tell you is how hard it can be to develop your comfort zone particularly, if, you are an athlete who is on the edge of their physical limits, a business man who has costly consequences which ride on their actions, or someone who, has bad memories of previous attempts at pushing their comfort zone. We all have different skills, qualities, health, experiences and sensitiveness to risk that have shaped who we are. These are based on our beliefs but by slowly extending our comfort zone we can push to achieve things we would have only dreamt of this morning, last week, last month or even last year. The easy option is always to remind in your comfort zone because we crave comfort, but this can be very dangerous because we start too stagnant and not continue to grow. If our Journey toward pinnacle performance has stopped; we stop learning and growing. So the fact is that we have to always extend our comfort zone however slowly.

"Just keep swimming" – Dory (Finding Nemo)

So when you make a decision to do or try something outside of your comfort zone you will have feelings of apprehension as you are moving from somewhere that is comfortable and familiar to a place outside of your comfort zone where you will have the fear of the unknown (injury, embarrassment, failure, danger or other consequences) and this will make you anxious. These feelings are natural and should be expected. Also the good news is that these feelings can be managed and strategies used to lessen their impact.

"We keep moving forward, opening new doors, and doing new things, because we're curious and curiosity keeps leading us down new paths." - Walt Disney

This fear is a survival mechanism; if you are in a familiar and comfortable environment you understand what it takes to survive. Imagine as a cave man you know what you need to do in your cave and immediate surroundings and feel comfortable (as comfortable as you can be in a cave!). If you ventured out of this area you would become uncertain of what you know about the environment and what it takes to survive. This uncertainty still exists in the modern world where the caves and forest have been replaced with job roles, professions, towns and cities. This uncertainty maybe stopping you from moving forward on your Journey by preventing you from applying for a new job and getting out of the job you do not enjoy (You only stay in this job because it is familiar and comfortable despite you not enjoying it).

The need to stay in the comfort zone is due to the brain's primary function to insure you avoid injury and survive.

Unfortunately, the choice to remain in your comfort zone will mean you never reach your true potential or find out what you are capable of achieving. So if you want to change or grow, sooner or later you're going to have to deal with the uncomfortable feelings and take that step to stretch your comfort zone. As Jillian Michaels has said **"You need to get comfortable being uncomfortable!"**

"It's a dangerous business, going out your door. You step onto the road, and if you don't keep your feet, there's no telling where you might be swept off to." - Bilbo Bagging

Stretching your comfort zone can only be a good thing but this is not easy. It will make you appreciate what you have and the skills and strengths you have. Stretching your comfort zone will also motivate you to change, stop you getting stuck in a rut, stimulate brain activity, make you more resilient and increase your confidence.

"A dream is your creative vision for your life in the future. You must break out of your current comfort zone and become comfortable with the unfamiliar and the unknown." - Denis Waitley

Extending your comfort zone and learning

"A comfort zone is a beautiful place, but nothing ever grows there" - Unknown

As the name suggests a comfort zone is a place of comfort, we are able to survive with less effort. If we are in our comfort zone we are comfortable but we can't learn effectively. This is because we know everything we need to achieve our primary objective of survival in the immediate environment. Being in your comfort zone is easy as we know everything we need to but if this is the case then we don't need to learn anything new. Falling deeper into your comfort zone is easy to do and it's then easier to stay there because as Human Beings we have natural urges to seek out and stay in comfortable surroundings. However, to learn effectively we have to be consciously aware of this and push ourselves outside of comfort zone and into our **growth zone**. In the growth zone we are in our best position to learn and get stronger as things are difficult and challenging. Every time we enter the growth zone we learn something. Think of the body builder who has to increase the weight they are lifting to build muscle. If they stayed on the same weight growth of the muscle would eventually stop. So to get into your growth zone follow the steps below.

"You are always a student, never a master. You have to keep moving forward." - Conrad Hall

Steps to extend your comfort zone

Extending your comfort zone is defiantly not an easy process but to help you do this there is a 6 step process that will help you achieve success in stretching your comfort zone. The best way to show how to extend your comfort zone is through using a real life example of someone with a long term serious injury. Let's set the scene; post injury he dreams about doing the things he used to do before the injury (running, mountaineering, climbing, mountain biking etc.) but he is very tempted to stay inside his comfort zone where he is safe because he fears upsetting the injury and the resulting pain. He makes excuses not to push himself by busying himself with things inside his comfort zone. However he sometimes kids himself that he is going to try to move out of his comfort zone but really he is actually still within it and talks himself into staying within it. So our example needs to be aware that he is in his comfort zone and then start to work toward his growth zone.

Step 1: Become Aware and select an area of your life in which you want to stretch your comfort zone.

The first step of the process to extend your comfort zone is to recognize that you are stuck in a rut, have been in a safe place for too long or are too comfortable in your comfort zone. This is awareness again (so make sure you complete the awareness exercises in the book). The need to extend your comfort zone maybe shown in feelings of becoming stagnant, dissatisfied and not very interested in things; this is your **tipping point** to start the process but this is hard work (see the next section). So to improve your situation select an area where you want to improve (it is best to extend your comfort zone in small key sections to maximize success) and then slowly move toward the edge of you comfort zone and then move into your growth zone.

So our example needs to understand and recognize that he is in a rut and then he must consciously and slowly increase the amount of exercise the injury can stand before it aches and becomes uncomfortable to extend his comfort zone. He needs to push himself out of his comfort zone by doing a little more exercise each day to limit the pain.

Step 2: Give yourself small targets to work toward which link to the bigger goal.

Of course stretching and operating outside of your comfort zone should not mean you do anything too extreme. Any targets you set yourself should fall just outside our comfort zone and within our growth zone. Once you have achieved this target you have grown and your comfort zone is bigger than it was before.

The optimum zone to set targets in your 'growth zone', where challenges are beyond what you've previously done, but not so challenging that they terrify you.

The advice is always to start small and have steady and progressive targets that slowly develop your comfort zone by operating in your growth zone. Our example needs to take little steps of improvement, no matter how small rather than give up because of the discomfort caused by the injury. He needs to level his expectations and understand that he may not be able to do what he used to do but can certainly strive to get as close as he can to what he was like pre injury.

Our example he needs to set small manageable targets that slowly extend his comfort zone. His new targets could include daily dog walks to replace the mountaineering or small local road rides to replace the mountain biking.

Your Journey will have peaks and troughs so you should expect setbacks (the contents and strategies in this book will help to deal with the troughs), which is why small targets are necessary because small setbacks are easier to recover from.

Step 3: Identify positive reference points and use imagery to picture a successful outcome

An important precursor to any successful activity is to identify any positive reference points that you could use to reinforce the belief you need to undertake development in the growth zone. Have you been in a similar situation before? For example, have you, in the past given a talk in public where you had some level of success but are now in a position where your confidence is not what it was because you have got complacent and regressed into a smaller comfort zone?

When you have these positive reference points you need to imagine yourself being successful in your efforts by regularly revisiting them and the success you had. If you do this as you extend your comfort zone it will lessen the feelings of flight, anxiety and fear associated with extending your comfort zone. Within the visualization see yourself taking your desired action to slowly extend your comfort zone with everything you do going smoothly; with nothing bad happening to you. Imagine that only good and positive things happen to you when you are in your growth zone (there is more information on imagery and visualization in the pinnacle performance blog). If you don't have reference points to access you can still successfully visualize. This would be like a child visualizing winning a gold medal at the Olympics despite never being in an Olympic Games. Imagine the very best possible outcome of extending your comfort zone; like winning a gold medal at the Olympics. This will slowly start to develop a reference point you can use.

So in our example he can revisit his reference points of past experiences of mountain biking and mountaineering and then use these to visualize himself getting as close as he can to what he was doing pre-injury.

"If you're in a comfort zone, afraid to venture out, take heart,

read examples of where others have succeeded against the odds, use them to develop your strength and push your zone even just a little." – Richard Glynn

Step 4: Be mindful (back to awareness).

Extending your comfort zone requires you to achieve goals and targets. If you are not aware of the goals you have achieved then you may have fallen back into your comfort zone because you are not moving forward. As a result the key with any goal or target is to check regularly on your progress to achieving it, this will keep you in your growth zone. This takes us back to awareness. As we know to extend your comfort zone you need to be operating in your growth zone. To remain here you need goals and targets that are challenging but achievable.

If they are too easy you will remain in your comfort zone. If they are too hard you venture to far past your growth zone which will cause you to eventually retreat back into the safety and solace of your comfort zone because things are too difficult. So you need to check in (at least once a week) with your targets to check whether they are pitched correctly and are keeping you in your growth zone which will drive you forward on your Journey.

So as you step outside your comfort zone and stretch towards achieving your target pay attention to any discomfort that starts to arise. This maybe a sign that you are trying to retreat back into the safety of your comfort zone. If this is the case try to use positive self-talk* to rationalize your feelings for example:

'This feeling of worry is just my brain trying to keep me safe. I know I am only going to push myself a little therefore I cannot hurt myself a lot'

*There is more information on the pinnacle performance blog on effective goal setting and self-talk.

With regard to our example, each time he pushes the level of his comfort zone he would fear aggravating his injury which would cause him pain and discomfort. He would access his rehabilitation and the target he has set for it. When he is feeling strong enough he would step outside and move his attention away from any slightly uncomfortable sensations and instead focus on the target he has set. He would remain aware of how his body is feeling and expect some discomfort, but stay within manageable levels and divert his attention while he is in this uncomfortable growth zone. This is linked to controlling the contollables which is a section further on in this book.

Additional, while he is in his growth zone he would develop new positive reference points that will feed his beliefs on recovering from his injury, moving him towards enjoying the activities he once did (e.g. being outside and feeling the elements). He is closer to what he was pre injury than he was yesterday but not as close as he will be tomorrow. This will give him the courage to continue extending his comfort zone.

Step 5: Embrace the experience

If stretching your zone was a success and you achieved what you set out too, savor and reflect on the positive feelings that come from this achievement. Gain confidence from the positive experience and then think about planning your next stretch into your growth zone. If you suffered a setback and did not achieve the goal which would have extended your comfort zone, accept this setback, resolve yourself that you will recover from this and re-adjust your targets. Remember, the more you practice the above, the more your; skill, resilience, confidence level and comfortable you'll be. Embrace the fact that you have learnt something from the experience.

In our example, if the activity was a success the next day's efforts start with more confidence and strength. If not, and the pain returns, he can step back into his previous comfort zone, rest, recover and when he feels strong enough try again but realizing that he has learnt something about himself from the experiences he has had whilst being injured.

Step 6: Plan further stretches

The fantastic thing about extending your comfort zone is that once you start extending it can be difficult to come to a complete stop. Imagine getting on a rollercoaster at a fair ground, once you're on your on! So even if you are unable to grow in some areas or if you fail in where you were expecting to succeed you can always dust yourself down take time to recover and try again where you left off or try to stretch again in another area. This takes good awareness. The great thing is that extending your comfort zone is a constant ongoing process. It's truly fascinating because we are all capable of achieving more than we give ourselves credit for. This is the Journey to pinnacle performance.

A final strategy to help you to extend your comfort zone, which will also provide a valuable and strong positive reference point for your beliefs, is to make sure you make regular checks on what you have achieved. I recommend doing this monthly, quarterly and yearly. Write your achievements down so you can record what you have achieved. You will be amazed how much you can achieve in one week, one month, and one year. Think about what are you able to do now and complete or cope with that you couldn't a year ago? For example, I have set up and run my own business that I wouldn't have thought possible 18 months ago!

Here are some other suggestions of comfort zones you could look to extend and stretch:

- Look to change a routine or habit and find a different way to do it
- Study a new language
- Try and start an online business
- Take up a new sport or hobby
- Plan a holiday off the beaten trail

- Take up a challenge for charity
- Try the opposite actions to which you are comfortable with:

  - If you're sedentary find a physical activity you can try.
  - If you're active, read, relax or watch a movie.
  - If you just listen to rock music try classical music.
  - If you're shy try speaking in front of people.

Another great aspect about extending your comfort zone and spending time in your growth zone is that this causes you to grow in other areas. So growth in one area extends into other areas and these grow as well. You will be amazed at the effect this has on other areas of your life. So if your attempts in developing one comfort zone take a setback then look to develop new interests and expand other comfort zones you have in your life. Have you ever started an exercise program to find that your diet almost automatically improves alongside this? You have more energy so your productivity at work increases and you have more time for your family and friends? It has a massive snowball effect on every aspect of your life. Extend your comfort zone in one aspect and you extend in everything else.

Do not be satisfied to stay permanently in your comfort zone. By all means use it as a safe haven to retreat to when you do not feel strong enough to push your comfort zone but, as and when you feel able, take frequent steps to venture out even just a small way into your comfort zone. The experience of pushing your comfort zone will make you feel good about yourself and feel more motivated to try and push your zone even further.

Hard Work

Without hard work nothing is possible. The need to work hard was, and still is, essential for survival in any environment (think back to the cave man example again!) whether the environment is in a new job or out in the wilderness (a la Bear Grylls). Each environment has different requirements that you need to work hard in to ensure that you achieve, but you need to be aware of these requirements first. Hard work is underpinned by a strong belief around work ethic which is imperative for anyone wanting to move forward on their Journey toward achieving goals. If you work hard enough you WILL achieve your goals. Listen to any successful person in any environment and they will state that it was hard work that got them where they are.

For example, I have a belief that hard work is essential in any endeavor (hence why it's a key principle in this book!). This belief has come from my parents, particularly my dad who has always worked incredibly hard and this has been passed onto me through his interactions with me and my observations of him. I identified this belief when I completed the self-awareness exercises from the previous sections. This belief around hard work which was formed as a result of seeing my dad working tirelessly for many years in two jobs to support his family.

"The harder I work the more I live." - George Bernard Shaw

The development of a strong work ethic belief is one of the core principles on the Journey to pinnacle performance which ultimately leads to a competitive advantage, self-development, and success. This is because hard work naturally extends your comfort zone as you are pushing to achieve difficult goals and objectives. By doing this you are operating in your growth zone which will keep you moving forward. Maintaining and developing the building blocks highlighted in this book is hard work. For example, being aware of everything you need to be aware of is hard work; there is so much to focus on, arguably an infinite number (most are not under your control! – more on this in the next section). Good awareness highlights that hard work is a major principle to keep moving forward on your Journey.

Working on your beliefs and checking their influence is hard work especially as they have so much influence over everything we do. If they are not the beliefs we want it is hard work to change them, if you have positive beliefs it is hard work to maintain them. You can have strong positive beliefs but if there is no hard work then everything else is pointless so a strong positive belief for a good work ethic is needed. Finally maintaining balance with all the different aspects of your life is hard work; ask any working parent!

"Hard work is the price we must pay for success." – Vince Lombardi

Hard work should be a principle that we all utilize in every aspect of our lives yet we are bombarded by images from the media of people who appear to have success and have not worked hard to achieve it. The media have confused the concepts of success and celebrity. Success and hard work are interlinked but the perception, through the media, can be that celebrity is success and that success can come 'cheap' because they are a celebrity as a result of winning a reality TV show! The media don't show the hard work, the graft, and the failures that true success is built on as it wouldn't sell magazines or draw in viewers so hard work has fallen out of favor by some people but they still expect success. True success can only come with hard work so hard work has always been there and always will be.

You will get nowhere without hard work.

Hard work gave us an evolutionly advantage to survive and ultimately be successful. We should expect that there will always be difficulties in our Journey because there are too many things outside of our control that can and will affect us. Hard work allows us to deal with these difficulties and get through them by focusing on and working on the things within our control.

There are two things to consider with hard work. The first is that hard work is pointless unless you also work intelligently. This means you have to work hard on the right things at the right times, this means you need to be aware to understand what these things and when they need to be worked on. How many examples have we seen of people working incredibly hard in the "wrong jungle" for little or no reward? Additionally the second thing to consider is that there so there are so many distractions in the modern world that procrastination can easily sneak in (me very much included in this). With the invent of hand held smart phones before we realize we have spent 30 minutes chasing the red dot or a like or thumbs up on social media and the immediate gratification this brings or playing a game to get onto the next level!

"Nothing will work unless you do." – John Wooden

Ask any parent who has experienced a family day out to the seaside (or even a theme park!) about hard work. This can be magical day out when you work hard to control the things you can (control the controllables again) but could be a nightmare if you fail to work hard to control these. For example, (and this is not an exhaustive list!) you need to control the amount of sleep that both the parents and children get the night before. The food you eat before and the food you take will all have an influence. The plan you produce that has a plan B if the weather is inclement or the route you have chosen route is blocked by traffic (Every British Bank Holiday!). Built into this plan is how long the travelling will be to the destination and how much money you are likely to need are just some of the things that you can plan for.

So if you don't put the hard work and effort into the preparation of a trip to the seaside for your perfect family day out you are increasing the chances of it being a failure. You can't control road works and the weather but you can prepare for them to limit their influence.

"Nothing ever comes to one, which is worth having, except as a result of hard work." – Booker T. Washington

In today's global competitive environment working hard is regarded by any company and organization as evidence that you are ready for promotion, gaining bonuses and developing respect of other individuals. On a personal level hard work allows you to get more out of the experiences that you have. However this hard work must be in the right areas, at the right times and be congruent to your beliefs otherwise your balance will be affected and things will start to slide because you are not working hard on them. You need to work smart as well as hard!

"The harder I work the luckier I get" – Thomas Jefferson

What is the "Work Ethic" belief?

Work ethic is a personal belief that is based on putting considered effort into your performance in the roles, functions and duties you have in your life. It is also a belief that by working hard to do the best job possible will be essential for your Journey forward. The work ethic belief is a personal driver that demands you take pride in everything you do whilst at the same time placing trust into your ability. Furthermore, people who display a work ethic belief consider the quality of work they produce to be a reflection on them so therefore put time and effort into the work they produce.

As a leader in a performance environment I commonly look for evidence of a work ethic belief. I would look for evidence of work ethic by; being reliable, showing initiative, developing new processes, seeking new contacts, pursuing new skills and "going the extra mile" in the performance of duties.

How to increase the work ethic belief

You can increase your work ethic belief by assessing your current attitudes toward the plates you have to spin (balance and awareness again!) and looking for ways in which you can improve. As a starting point assess your skills in the following areas:

1. Showing Good Personal Administration

One of the easiest skills to develop and is most effective at showing this belief is to get organized and develop your time management skills (there will be more on this on the pinnacle performance blog and in future books in the series, in meantime I would again recommend you to read David Allen's book called Getting Things Done). Work on getting organized and getting things done (this will extend your comfort zone as well).

Work to be on time to work, a meeting or appointment. Try to get up a few minutes earlier, try to anticipate delays and unexpected incidents on your way to work. Communication that is open is the key here so always attempt to inform those involved if you expect to be absent or delayed because even the most organized and prepared person will occasionally be late because of factors outside of their control (It happens to the best of us!). What they can control is how they respond to these factors and communicate effectively about how they are affected by them.

If possible, it is best to work on arriving to appointments early to ensure that time is used appropriately and hard work can happen.

2. Demonstrate a positive, problem-solving and helpful approach.

People, who stay focused on the job, try to solve setbacks and adapt to changes by making themselves control the controllables become indispensable. This could be indispensable to the organization they work for, the team they play for or from an individual perspective show a positive and problem solving approach to their Journey.

This approach is assisted by discipline, having a focus on quality and showing a sense of responsibility.

Discipline

Show good discipline by staying focused on the building blocks and the principles outlined in this book. Work hard to extend your comfort zone to achieve your goals by focusing on things under your control by staying determined to maintain balance, and by developing awareness and positive beliefs. Personal discipline is an essential quality in developing professionalism.

Committed to Quality

It is not enough to produce the bare minimum; this will eventually cause your Journey to pinnacle performance to stop. You will start to stagnate which is not a good place to be so a commitment to quality will help you to always produce more than you need to.

Be willing to read into and work on the subjects that are important for your Journey. This involves awareness again! The first major subject is to focus on you, you are the most important subject, so consider what your strengths, goals and interests are so you can identify publications to read around the subject to become a 'mini expert' in them. Also start to read self-development books to improve different qualities in yourself that will support your Journey. Do this whilst reading around your other subjects.

Also, make sure you examine how others have completed the things you are involved in whether that is a certain profession or business and become aware of others who you are competing against so you can consider what improvements you can make. Do your best to produce work that is fit for purpose and exceeds expectations in every aspect of your life, always look for improvements you can make.

"Success is dependent upon the glands – sweat glands." - Zig Ziglar

Show a Sense of Responsibility

"I don't think of myself as a poor deprived ghetto girl who made good. I think of myself as somebody who from an early age knew I was responsible for myself, and I had to make good." - Oprah Winfrey

Showing a sense of responsibility is closely linked to the next section on controlling the controllables as you are solely responsible for all the things under your control and this sense of responsibility will affect how hard you work. So always work hard on these things and take responsibility for them. This means you need to be aware of and maintain good balance that is right for you to keep everything going to move forward. You are accountable for them, it is up to you!

Although it will not be easy (and will be hard work!) to master all of the above practicing them will make you feel good about yourself, by getting a grip, taking responsibility and taking charge of your Journey. It will give you a focus, something that is in your control and allow you to extend your comfort zone.

Hard work will have a significant impact on your future success.

"Go forward with a great desire forever beating at the door of our hearts as we travel toward our distant goal." - Helen Keller

"Life is 10% what happens to you and 90% how you react to it"– Charles R. Swindoll

Whoever you are, when an uncontrollable circumstance hits it can be very difficult to accept and manage. For example, if you have been affected by a sudden major event it is always difficult to deal with in the immediate aftermath of the news breaking. I describe this feeling as 'it's always worse in the bubble'. What this means is that it is worse in the moment but looking back after the event you have grown, learnt something from the experience and have the ability to better manage this event/situation if it was to occur again; it's not as difficult as when it originally happened. Think about the time you fell over and scrapped your knee as a child. The immediate pain and discomfort was high which was difficult to accept but as the healing began the pain started too subsided with the pain being not as bad as when you initially fell. This is natural but the only way is to manage this circumstance is to control the controllables.

This is hard work (as with everything in this book!) because there are so many things that are uncontrollable. This list of uncontrollable things could be considered endless so the only logical method to deal with this is to only really focus on the things under your control. This focus on things on under your control is the only way to move forward on your Journey. You need to be aware of uncontrollable things and how you react to them but the focus has to be inward and to things you are responsible for. When you are driving a car you control the accelerator (under your control) otherwise you wouldn't go anywhere but you have to be aware of other drivers (outside of your control) on the road so you can react (under your control) appropriately to them if required.

Looking at uncontrollable things in your environment will take you away from the things that will really get you through the difficult times whilst distracting you from the Journey. For example, if you need to achieve a qualification to get that promotion at work then you need to focus on the things within your control to achieve this; things like how much hard work is needed to complete it, how can you balance everything already in your life and how can you afford to pay for it. Everything else should be disregarded.

The human tendency to focus on uncontrollable things could be an evolutionary throwback from our distant past. The environment our ancient ancestors lived in had so many things that could affect the survival chances of them (e.g. a Sabre Toothed Tiger walking around the corner and into your cave or an earthquake to name just a few!!). With so many factors this would cause high levels of fear which in turn would cause our ancestors to stay alert and to be constantly on their toes which would increase their chances of survival as they could react to circumstances when they were presented with them. This mentality is very much still here, we still have a tendency to have an external focus on the things we cannot control.

So when we experience an uncontrollable circumstance it is very easy to concentrate on the external factors because they present themselves as being the immediate problems we need to deal with but in reality the only way to deal with it is to control the controllables. If you focus on trying to change the uncontrollable external factors you will fail *as* King Canute did when he tried to command the tide of the sea to stop coming in. So your focus should instead be on what you can affect, on what you can control. This changes your perspective and attitude to a positive can do attitude which will push your forward on your Journey.

For example, if you suffer from bouts of frequent pain from an old injury (like our example from the extending your comfort zone section), then the pain could spoil your daily outlook. You cannot stop the pain and so it is an uncontrollable. The pain is only something you can influence. This means that you can do things to minimize its impact like following the instructions/exercises prescribed by a physiotherapist or health professional. You can also change your focus away from the injury to more positive pursuits. If, however, you keep busy and focus on other things the concentration on the pain moves to other things that you can affect like the effort you put into work and the family life. Thus, you are in control by changing your outlook to a more positive one.

"Your attitude to the situation is the first thing you can affect"

We are not advocating completely ignoring the uncontrollables but to be aware of them and to recognize which are totally out of your control and should be immediately ignored (like the weather); these factors that you can't control but are under your influence are how you react to them (like wearing appropriate clothing for the conditions). You need to concentrate on the things in your control as a priority and then after these have been completed look at those factors that you can influence.

"There is no such thing as bad weather - only the wrong clothes"– Billy Connolly

Steps to Controlling the Controllables

Here are three steps to help you chart a course through difficult waters and to keep moving forward on your Journey by controlling the controllables.

Step 1:
You have to tighten the belt and **become more aware, understand and then accept you are where you are.** This will allow you to **recognize what factors about your current situation you cannot affect or change and which are within your control.** Complete the awareness exercises presented earlier in the book. By working in you circle of influence (taken from Stephen Covey's book, 7 Habits of Highly Effective People)

you will continue to move forward however slow. Moving forward slowly is better than not moving at all.

"It does not matter how slowly you go as long as you do not stop."- Confucius

There are a number of examples of people who have been involved in accidents or have been stuck in the wilderness which has caused them to go to extreme lengths (like cutting their own broken arm off with a 2" pen knife) to survive. They did this by being aware and then taking control of the situation by focusing on the things within their control. This is the ultimate example of controlling the controllables to continue on your Journey.

Embrace the challenge of the situation you are in. Think of the sportsmen who always have to compete for a win, soldiers who have to fight to succeed and great businessmen that have taken ailing companies and had to take huge financial risks to develop profitability, families who have had to survive in times of famine or uncertainty. All of these examples have controlled the controllables and worked within their circle of influence; they have maintained positive beliefs (under their control) and become more aware of what they can control and what they can't.

Prepare yourself for the strain you will inevitably feel from the uncontrollable circumstance you are in; bend with the wind, retreat or regroup, divert your mind, present a leading edge to the wind, shelter from the storm. Take whichever action is under your control, which is within your circle of influence and necessary for you to, first survive. From here you can re-evaluate your position (awareness again) where you can develop an inner calm because you can focus on the things you have at your disposal and have considered how you can be proactive to move forward in the situation you are in.

Another example on controlling the controllables is a military one from the Falklands war when a Royal Marine carrying full kit was asked by a reporter "how far are you carrying that pack?" The Royal Marine replied "As far as they tell me!" The Royal Marine controlled the things he could control in this situation which was his mindset and failed to have his focus drawn externally on the distance he was expected to travel with full kit over difficult terrain in very tough weather.

"Reduce the impact of the pressure you feel from the uncontrollable by planning how you will react by using the resources you have in your control"

Step 2:

The ability to plan and think ahead is under your control so **plan** your best course of action to survive the difficult times and prepare to ride out the things that are out of our control by focusing on the things we can control. You need to play with the occasion not against it. Run with the wind, ride the wave, shelter from the storm. Make sure you play to win as opposed playing not to lose. Surround yourself with positive influences, seek positive beliefs and plan how you will survive (all within your control!). Put all your resources into that plan and develop it at every opportunity (again within our control!).

"Play to Win, be prepared to play the long game"

Step 3:

Always prepare for better times, weather changes, tides change, economies runs in cycles, pain eases, and competition constantly changes. These are all external and ultimately outside of our control, we can only control our reaction to these. All these examples are cycles and **everything** in nature runs in cycles so an awareness of this is important of what needs to be completed at particular stages of the cycle. A farmer along with his family would go hungry in autumn and winter if he did not tend to the soil and plant seeds in spring and then in summer didn't look after the growing crop. For the farmer this is hard work but the work he puts in is within his control so he can influence as much as possible the cycle of the seasons so he has a supply of food for his family.

"It's a round world"– David Beckham

Our modern way of living has taken us away from these cycles so we need to re-familiarize ourselves with them and become aware that cycles happen so bad times will always eventually turn to good times. We have to be aware that we can't control these cycles but we can influence our reaction to them. This all starts with your building blocks of pinnacle performance and the other principles of hard work and extending your comfort zone. You become aware of the environment and control the things you can control within this, work hard to extend your comfort zone and develop positive beliefs. Doing this will influence your reaction to the cycle you find yourself in. You have worked within your circle of influence to illicit a positive change in the cycle you find yourself in.

So it makes sense to use times of downturn to prepare for when things improve, to concentrate on developing the areas that are within your control so you are ready for an upturn and the positive change in the cycle.

In summary to control the controllables you have to answer and act on these three questions:

What is out of my control? – Do not try to affect or concentrate on this. Do not get into a negative mindset.

What do I control? – Develop a positive mindset embrace the controllables and put all your efforts into achieving them.

What is the plan? - Work within you circle of influence to produce a plan to first survive and stop the slide and then to immediately and however fast move forward in the future. You can do this by using achievable targeting by completing the Next Action thinking exercises in this book.

Military Basic Training Example (by Richard Glynn)

This example outlines how the military use the essential building blocks and principles of pinnacle performance highlighted in this book to achieve the highest possible levels of success within the tough environment that is Basic Military Training (BMT). This was my (Richies) first introduction to understanding the need for strong foundations in terms of the building blocks and principles and their importance in reaching our true potential.

BMT is designed to ensure it created successful combat personnel capable of operating in difficult and extreme environments in as short a time frame as possible. It achieves this by developing the building blocks of pinnacle performance of **Awareness, Belief** and **Balance** as well as the principles of **Extending your Comfort Zone, Hard Work** and **Controlling the Controllables**. Without these being in place success in BMT cannot be achieved.

BMT is a progressive training program where the military take individuals as the raw material and develops their potential through a series of phases. Each service has slight differences in its training but the ethos and principle is shared between services. BMT is seriously underestimated by most recruits and is a very challenging and demanding course. Instructional staff train and test recruits to simulate a combat environment that tests both mental and physical resilience. The failure rate can be high but those who are successful will emerge better equipped to survive further training and military life in general. My intake started with thirty people and finished with twenty. The pace was fast and if you didn't do your share of the work - you were sent packing!

The first six weeks were an introductory phase which gives recruits their first introductions to military life and what will be required of them. Covering subjects such as: Values & Standards,

Physical Training, Skill at Arms, Drill and Field craft. The first objective in BMT is to ensure the recruit becomes **aware** of the expected objectives and how they fall short both as individuals and as a team. Drill Sergeants shout instructions, and everything is carried out at a fast pace. Early mornings, late nights, kit inspections, cleaning, polishing, physical tiredness is part of everyday life.

BMT is designed to make new recruits more aware of the individual and group goals that need to be achieved and the need to achieve them as a team. Instant directed feedback from the staff is used to ensure all recruits understand and practice the importance of group thinking, action and reflection.

New Recruits will remain in barracks for the duration of this phase helping them to develop as a group and become aware of each other's strengths and weaknesses. Recruits usually find some difficulty becoming accustomed to a new way of life and become aware of the gravity of their decision to join and also the support which is available from fellow recruits, the drill staff and the service they are hoping to join.

This leads onto the second principle that runs throughout the BMT which is **hard work**. Basic Training is viewed as a life changing Journey with clearly identified stages which need to be achieved; these become your daily focus. The service ensures all recruits are challenged in relation to their ability making sure each stage is difficult but achievable.

My favorite memories from these weeks are crawling around in the snow and the tough but progressive physical training sessions. I also started to become aware how much I enjoyed the company of fellow recruits, the challenge of the training and how committed I was to complete it. I also have memories of log races and stretcher carries which were intense and gave a real insight of what was to come. The entire group was utterly exhausted, legs felt the heaviest that they had ever been and we struggled to keep up the pace.

The third principle within BMT is to **extend your comfort zone**; taking you from a point of being comfortable to a place beyond this, as I have already mentioned training staff were experts in defining each recruits strengths and weaknesses. Each individual was extended to the point of ensuring they were operating well beyond their comfort zone but still within their growth zone. Each recruit certainly feels they have had to dig deep into physical, mental and emotional reserves to complete the training.

Instructors would constantly push you on the assault course and always demanded you to give your best effort. Endless rifle, first aid, marching and parade drills would need to be memorized, protocols and procedures would need to be practiced and carried out under pressure. Effort rather than ability was used as the measure; each recruit was expected to give 100%. Two mile speed marches in full kit and carrying weapons are used to test recruits to the limit. Instructors set off at a fast pace over a tough course with significant hills. They ensured all recruits needed to work at their individual maximum to keep the pace.

In this way BMT unlocks reserves of stamina and endurance you did not realize you possessed. The principle of extending your comfort zone is a powerful principle in your Journey to complete BMT and your military career beyond that. BMT encourages you to actively seek the edge of your comfort zone and then go that one step or even two steps further. The military recognize this is the only way you can improve.

Being aware what needs to be achieved is extremely important but is useless unless you **believe** you can achieve. BMT recognizes that self-belief determines the amount of effort recruits expend in working towards achieving each stage in training. BMT also recognizes there may be limiting beliefs that slow recruits down or even stop them achieving. All instructional staff recognize the power that positive and strong beliefs have in

The Sheffield College

Hillsborough LRC
Telephone: 0114 260 2254

driving recruits forward. All BMT staff are selected on their length of military experience as well as their coaching and instructional abilities. Staff encourage all recruits to develop self-reliance, self-belief and coping strategies at all stages of the training.

I have already mentioned how BMT uses drills to teach new skills, without the use of drills to aid memory, develop conditioning and quick correct actions the training, in such short periods of time would not be possible. BMT looks to develop "flow", smoothness and efficiency in recruits' actions. During BMT every activity is broken down into small component parts and each is taught and added too until the activity is understood. Then the activity is practiced time and time again until it becomes second nature. It is at this point that **balance** is achieved. Without balance being achieved during BMT the recruits would not be able to retain the knowledge gained and operate effectively in other areas of their life outside of BMT. Instructors encourage recruits to develop balance through the delivery of constructive feedback, questioning the recruits' decision making and encouraging them through difficult times.

The final principle which recruits learn during BMT is the ability to **control the controllables**. This sounds easier than it actually is because there is tendency to focus on the external factors within the environment of BMT. BMT trains recruits to look at everything outside of their control as irrelevant so the focus has to be only on the things under your control with the main one being your beliefs. They are taught to understand that time and energy spent on these factors will be wasted and should instead be used on the things you can control to keep you moving toward your goal of being successful within BMT. Recruits are taught phrases like, "we are where we are" and "solider on" to help them remember to think of living in the "here and now" and to focus on facts rather than emotion to help them keep moving forward whatever situation they find themselves in. They are encouraged to look at all times on what they can do to improve their situation rather than what they wish they could do.

BMT helps recruits to develop their ability to control the controllables by taking every recruit past their physical limits during the final weeks. BMT throws a final physical challenge to the would-be recruits which demands that they perform all they have been taught but under extreme pressure. The final exercise takes the form of a long route march with testing mental situations to master as a team on route. This final exercise is ten miles in three hours, carrying a 37 pound Bergan and a rifle. What makes this event a challenge is the fatigue from the previous days. I felt like my legs weighed a ton and that was before we even got started!

This final task is impossible to achieve as an individual and is only possible if all recruits act as one. It is during this period of training that you really bond with your fellow recruits, relying on each other to get through it all.

The physical and mental effort needed to achieve this exercise is huge "I felt like my legs were like lead weights and my lungs would explode." The only way through this is to focus on your goal and keep putting one leg in front of the other, rely on your team mates to help you, help them, hold on and keep going till you achieve your goal. In other words focus on your body, mind and the goal. These are all things you can control and it is these factors which you should focus on not: negative emotion, pain, discomfort, the situation, environment and weather all of which cannot be controlled.

The phase ends with the recruits taking part in a pass out parade, receiving their berets, posting orders to trade training and a long weekend off. However, if recruits have managed to pass BMT they have proved to the military that they have developed the building blocks of Awareness, Belief and Balance as well as the principles of Extending your Comfort Zone, Hard Work and Controlling the Controllables. Without these being in place success in BMT cannot be achieved and the military can be sure each recruit will have the essential building blocks and principles needed to see them successfully through further military training and a life in the Armed Forces.

Together the building blocks and principles during BMT form the recruits "Inner Core". The military believe the "inner core" influences absolutely everything that you do; it dictates your actions and behaviors and is essential in developing robust and service personnel. I would certainly rate BMT as one of the best experiences in my life, especially when I was given a fly past watched by my parents on the final parade. I feel extremely honored to have belonged to the military and to have worked with some of the most professional and skilled personnel I have ever known and would recommend it to anyone who is looking for challenge in their lives.

This book is on the Building Blocks and Principles needed to propel you forward on your Journey. This book is the first in a series of books around what is needed to be a winner and be successful. In the pinnacle performance book series we will outline and demonstrate our pinnacle performance model we have developed. The first part of this model is the contents of this book; the Journey with the Building Blocks and Principles needed to be successful. Together we call the Building Blocks and Principles highlighted in this book the *Inner Core*. As we know your inner core influences absolutely everything that you do; it dictates all of your *actions and behaviors*. If we can work on these Building Blocks and Principles then you are moving forward on your Journey to pinnacle performance. Understanding effect of the inner core on your Journey is key.

Our model has different levels that are all influenced by the Building Block and Principles highlighted in the Inner Core. Imagine our model to resemble an onion or the Earth's crust with different layers but all ultimately controlled by the inner core. This is similar to the pinnacle performance model; all actions have consequences which we then deal with using our inner core. Therefore it is essential that you work to develop your inner core. The good news is the inner core can be developed and improved by completing the activities within this book but it takes time. Use this book as a reference tool and dip in and out as you need to.

We hope you have enjoyed this book and it will prove a valuable resource on your Journey toward PINNACLE PERFORMANCE!

References

Here are the references used in the book. I would recommend each of these as an essential addition to any library (as well as this one!) for your Journey.

Allen, D. (2001). *Getting Things Done: The Art of Stress-Free Productivity.*

Covey, S.R. (2004). *The Habits of Highly Effective People.*

Robbins, A. (2001). *Awaken the Giant within.*